HONEY IN THE LION

COLLECTED POEMS

Doris B. Gold

BIBLIO PRESS

All Rights Reserved
Copyright © Doris B. Gold 1979

Acknowledgments

Several poems in this collection have appeared in:
*The Tiger's Eye, Experiment, Accent, Kansas Quarterly,
The Writer, Freshtones,* an anthology, NYC Intercollegiate
PULSE, St. Louis Poetry Center, *Washington University
Magazine, CORE* Anthology, Colorado Poetry Society,
New Masses, and *Observer/Kaleidoscope* at Brooklyn
College, where the Department of English Prize in Poetry
was awarded in 1946.

Some poems were the basis for the Alexander Carruth Poetry
Award at the University of Kansas, Lawrence, 1948.

Cover: A Lion, by Rembrandt. In the Louvre, Paris.

ISBN 0-9602036-1-3

Library of Congress Catalog no. 78-73259

 Produced at The Print Center, Inc., Box 1050, Brooklyn, N.Y., 11202, a non-profit printing facility for literary and arts-related publications. Funded by The New York State Council on the Arts and the National Endowment for the Arts.

BIBLIO PRESS
P.O. Box 22
Fresh Meadows, N.Y. 11365

TABLE OF CONTENTS

RESPONSE 7
HIM 8
BIRTHDAY 9
LIFE STYLE 10
POEMS FOR NEW YORK CITY 11
SPEECH TO SENIOR CITIZENS 14
DAWN JOURNEY: SUBURBIA 16
STREET CRY 18
APOLLO 14 19
THE ERL-KING 20
AT CHANUKAH 21
CHILD AT THE PIANO 22
THREE BARS FOR JOHN CAGE 23
GENRE PICTURE 24
HESPED 25
COUSINS' CLUB 27
MEMORIAM 28
BY THE SEA 29
WASTREL 30
THE PLEASURE OF BEING HUMAN 31
THE FAMILY AT THE FALLOUT SHELTER 32
ABOARD THE HONEY FITZ 33
ABSOLUTION 34
AUTUMN AGE 35
STUTTERER 36
VALSE TRISTE 37
SCRIPT FOR THE I.R.T. 38

TRIPTYCH FOR TALMUD TORAHS 39
FOURTH OF JULY 42
SEND FORTH A RAVEN 43
RADICAL SPEECH 44
THEME FOR A SINGLE GIRL 45
ALBUM 46
ENEMIES 47
ANTHEM FOR 1950 48
BLUES SONG 49
TRAVEL 51
PORTRAIT OF HAROLD 52
PICASSO STILL LIFE 53
JOURNEYSONG 55
NIGHT STEPS 57
ESQUIRE HILL 58
NUPTIALSONG 59
OUTSIDER 60
SUNDAY 61
A SUITE TO SCHOLARS 63
NEW POET TO OLD 69
LOVE POEM 71
A PICTURE FROM ITALY 72
SPACE AGE 74
OVER A BRIDGE 75
TIMES SQUARE 76
LINES AT TWENTY-SIX 77
A HAMMER FOR THE WISE MAN 78
TIME OUT OF JOINT 80

... and he turned aside to see the carcass of the lion; and, behold, there was a swarm of bees and honey in the carcass of the lion.

And Samson said unto them, I will now put forth a riddle unto you: And he said unto them, Out of the eater came forth meat, and out of the strong came forth sweetness.

Judges 15

RESPONSE

That out of the body of feared strength,
The lion of father of my fathers,
Where the Ark shows the sign to us,
Should be the nest of bees
In which I am one in name.*

Riddle of appearance,
That the lion asks with his eyes
For other becoming, and cannot.
That bees might beget butterflies,
But habitate honeycombs.

Honey in the lion,
The living part of death,
My mother and father natures
And their ancient body breath
Grows in mine.
How sweet the song may be/become,
How strong the thought/the answers.

Audacity of life:
The possibility of finding and of loss,
I speak of Them,
I am Thou,
Saying Yes and No in meeting,
An answer.

*Dvorah, meaning a bee, is the Hebrew name for Doris.

See *The Way of Response* by Martin Buber.

HIM

The last I saw you,
I was unseen,
As in a dream,
Fearing revelation.

You dressed in white,
(As always, your innocence)
The brows were grey,
And so the stubble on the face.
Bare used arms,
But still unburdened back;
The years only a slight bruise.
You wore sneakers.
Your head like the David of Michelangelo,
Was now the color of aluminum.

People shuffled by,
The air sing-songing in that Coney carnival.
Your eyes were on your hands,
Not distancing the shore
Like a captain's gaze,
As once remembered.
The sound of tides nearby
Recalled our rush of sentences.

Descended from the temple frieze,
And disguised in that marketplace,
I saw you fumbling in the trash for newspapers.

1978

BIRTHDAY

Innocent in the afternoon,
A woman dusts the edge of mirrors.

A cut of pain; blood writes a signature.
The skin is opened like an eyelid.
There lies the red essence,
A piece of self revealed.

A drumming in the flesh
Affirms familiar breath.

Like a primitive,
The body is notched,
Ready for the dance of time,
The passage of left hours or years.

1977

LIFE STYLE

My grandmother in her frame
Oversees my kitchen,
All checkered brown and white.

The color of her immigrant ship is now mine.
Here are her marriage candlesticks,
Her pickle jugs, her blue bent pots inherited.
I use her antique spoons.
Soup overflows,
Boiled eggs are drumming.
The furnace of my home
Is stoked like hers.
The onion peel wakes memory
Of her menthol scent,
Her balm for pain and rage.
(A husband strange,
The shame of poverty)

My snakeplants shoot up swords,
Pieces of her toughness.

She is a household god
Who will not be denied.
But I see her Bohemian eyes in mine,
And hear the playing of zithers.

1976

POEMS FOR NEW YORK CITY

1.

We stay
At the edge of land.
Work, walk and sleep
In the city
Shaped like folds of taffeta.
The boros lying like shadows
That crook and curve
To find the ocean.

Robe of our ancients,
Beautiful as Pocahontas
Or Columbus's collar,
We wear you to festivals and funerals,
Parades and sails.

Not four hundred,
But a thousand years
It took to elevate our bones.
We rise to meet the monoliths
We dare to kiss as home,
Glowing in the night
Like immortal ash.

The scream of future hope
From all our throats,
The birth cries of repeated dawns.
Never the pyre of funerals
That jealous men
Bound to earth
Would immolate.

2.

We have become a country,
Not a page but a book.
A mile for every day in the year,
Red city on the mouth of Hudson.

Verazzano and Minuit memories,
Your cargo increaseth.
Millions packed in the hold,
Footfalls of nations
Ride, run, swarm toward us.

Five apples on a stick,
Honeyed, green, flecked, bruised,
Tough stemmed,
Hanging on the world's bough.

Planes like bows on strings
Pitch the urban orchestra,
Railroads cross us like cats' cradles.
Ships moo and fart in our harbor.

Badges, the flowers of authority
Bloom on chests,
The evenings brood;
Brows are lowered; hands itch.

Cabs race to harvest minutes;
Dollars fall like snow in Wall Street.
Mother of mazes,
We live in hives of houses
Like glorious insects.

Comfortable as Queens,
Wounded by fire and water in the Bronx,
Rich in dead as an Indian Mound,*
Tuning and babbling as a Brooklyn band,
An island of hated men hatted.

Here is that place
Where natives chant,
The king is dead; long live the king!

1976

―――――

*boro of Richmond.

SPEECH TO SENIOR CITIZENS

Say, you bag-draggers, moneysitters, criers and disdainers,
Say, you cheerers, dreamers, glad-handers, homesitters;
Prepare not the bankbook gift for your children,
The proper clothes in the closet,
The catered funeral.

Keep moving,
Let death hide-and-seek you
In the wood, hugging ancient trees,
Sitting in the shade of your minutes,
Looking for clovers.
Illness the weed is hidden in the green.

Play ping-pong with hours,
The holidays as trophies.
Finish the hoarding and hiding,
Fear of slippery weather,
Quest for medicine bargains.

Go migratory on planes,
Buses and cars.
Even at twilight meet muggers,
Outstare them, touch your whistle.

To your durable coat,
Add striped scarves.
Cherish your head in berets.
Bright gloves give hands power.
Kiss on lips again,
Inhale odors of women and men,
Their sweat and their sex.

Prepare not for perpetuity,
Crowd your space
Before you pay the landlord of the universe.
Breathe deep. Exhale.
Place candles in the crown of life.

1975

DAWN JOURNEY: SUBURBIA

Still night.
I await news of a condition,
As in a hospital.
The shoulder of the hill turns in sleep,
The blue dawn hiding the snow ghost
Whispers dread tales to children.

The moon like a watchcase
Ticks the time of night.
Street stores glow
Like final ash.
The night heaves in hibernation.

The Dipper waits for the cup of day
To pour, then empties as light limns the trees.
The wind makes a spitting sound over the river
Snaking its way to the city.

Here I stand,
Like my father expecting his ship,
My mother her operations.
My grandparents ready with horses
On the roads of Russia.
I too have waited trains,
Playing scenes of survival
In the leap of space,
Before this commuter run
To a desk in a skyscraper.

It is coming.
First a beam bouncing on the road;
A game machine.
Then an incandescent icicle
Moves to meet my feet.
The bosom of the bus is here.
It opens to receive my head, my body.
Together we leave home.

1975

STREET CRY

Who will buy the songs?
Who will read the poems?
   They cry the wail of wrongs,
   But there is honey in the combs.

Who will hear the songs?
Who will speak the poems,
   They strike the hour long,
   To you in idle domes.

Buy some songs today!
Read the poems tomorrow!
   The work of hands you passers pay,
   But not the truth of song,
      And more's the sorrow.

Who will buy the songs?
Who will read the poems?
   They shout the joy of young,
   They call the cry of crones.

Who will hear the songs?
Who will speak the poems?
   Those who beat the gongs?
   They who buzz like drones?

Buy some songs today—
Speak the poems tomorrow—
   All in the marketplace say Nay,
   Tin and copper wares they follow.

Then do not buy the songs,
And turn away the poems—
   For you who never seek or long,
   The only verse is carved on stones!

APOLLO 14

Ghosts of the Renaissance,
Spectral rose of mountain climbers.
Like Peary at the cold pole,
Millions in the stadiums of screens
Watch the feat like football.
Veterans of sky wars
With Boyscout patches at their hearts,
Spell out the play of astral games.

Table of the universe
Set with hardware on moonwhite
Kangaroo leaps over aeons to futurity.
Like idols of past belief
A shibboleth for witness stands:
A flag to claim the craters,
Starched for piety and proclamation,
Like Protestants in church mark heaven.

Antares, bright star,
Lights the cavern of the sky
For forty-niners chipping rock,
The search for scientific gold,
Saying, "Baby, baby..."

Fathers of work and duty
Plant their kiss on friend of earth,
The Moon.
Puppets of technology,
With string umbilicus for breath.
Gnomes or Brothers in a cowl of white,
Kittyhawk the protein in their genes.

At Delphi the python slain;
Now become the pure Helios.
We see the century in Phoebus Apollo.
What prophecy? The flock waits.

Earthshine is in the seer's eyes;
The dream dissolves; the real remains.

1971

THE ERL-KING*

Into my ear you speak messages,
Flung back from the wild space of years.

I hear of the changes:
An end to diligence;
The money-mongering.
Was it that Art deserted him or he it?
The peripety and philosophy in parks,
His potion for the young,
Yielded now to paper, paste and measure.

How he is shorn like Samson
By a brute Delilah!
And silence, like a blindness
Makes a cave of his mouth.
Prophet and teacher, is your speech held,
Whose words turned like the spectrum
Of daylight until the nights of our youth.

"My father, my father" I call to him.
Only the willow of memory moves.

The Erl-King has fallen from the speeding horse of life!
The daughters have wived;
The sons are disciples of jobs;
All are safe in their bosoms.

He is mortal;
The children are uncharmed.

1970

*See Schiller's poem of the same title.

AT CHANUKAH

As goodly as Catholics to their Christmas church
Would we go in Sabbath best to *shul*.*
Flame in the lab of faith
Ignites in careless chemistry.
Our bearded fathers burned the argument
On the match of minds.
Now we look out on the street
Beyond our eight window candles
And chant lamentations for the history.

At night the lights like lips in speech
Speak quietly the tongue of Gentiles.
The bosom of the neighborhood is proud,
Orange bulbs uniting all.

That each should have his place,
And piety the scent to please the Puritans,
We stay in our tents of Abraham,
Lifting the flap of family
And not the golden door of Rome.

Ourselves both host and traveller,
The charity we give is shelter to our souls
Fleeing the deserts,
Finding ease in Zion
Until another time of Maccabees.

1968

---

*shul is the Yiddish vernacular for synagogue.

CHILD AT THE PIANO

Gloves on thumbs
And dropping pebbles.
Notes are aim for beanshooters;
Sharps and flats are neuter.
All is music for a mother's hum
And breaking the bread of silence.

Fingers weave the days of growing
On the loom of piano keys. . .
A life machine;
But first, his bicycle.

1967

THREE BARS FOR JOHN CAGE

for electronic   Not for him the cry against the lost
instruments   Eden.
                                       His nucleus bombarded,
                                       A cell of matter is the man.

Pitch above high D
on audiometer   His wires make noises, not his soul;
                                          a new Neanderthal.
                                  Primitive of the steel age,
Modulate 7 turns   trapped in technology,
on the oscilloscope   He is the slave
for low and high   Held by its magnetic ray
static   In a love dance with gears.

Grate pebbles   Soon the singing throat will disappear.
And flower pots   Science will silence orchestras.
with tuning fork   Dials will dance.

Immerse a bell   Instead plucked wires resounding
In water. Lift up   Will hum like nervous blood
     and ring once.   The requiem of humanness.
Thud a boot twice.

1963

GENRE PICTURE

While artists paint and cry their strife,
We women have our Chardin jugs of cream,
Our antique bowls and oranges:
Of these we make still lives.

The palette of a wife
Shades from goods bestowed and bought,
The crude freight of family
Treasured for a certain knife.

Mops are brushes and the water oil,
We dip and daub; home quivers in the light;
The threshhold has a face of art
That bears its human soil.

Ceramics in repose are here
Forever waiting their refill,
The shelf sags with its storebought glass
Less meant for wine than beer.

Sheets fold rich when turning beds,
Drapes at evening clothe the body night;
Cloths are for the spill of soup and fruit,
Imprimatur of being fed.

We are La Gioconda at the pepper mill;
Ours are Picasso's eyes for merchandise,
The Rembrandt light of self falls dim
But bright are the artifacts in lives so still.

Student of sight,
Look well into the lens,
See that art and life are things;
Not what the heart intends.

1962

HESPED*

after the *Lamentations* of Jeremiah
for my mother, Goldie Bauman, 1891–1961

They are chopping down trees
In the heart's wilderness.
Woodsman, stay the stump and all its
Alien roots. The bitter fruit is down.
The apples never sunned
Merge green on distant grass.

I seek my meat where I should mourn;
Behold you were my mother's name,
And I the child of thwart
Was never comforter, and judged you
Solemn because your yoke was borne.

You were the first of six,
Mismated seed, no doubt for duty's sake begat.
The martyred eyes accuse in purple photographs
Now willed to me. A prisoner of fear
Within the cell of poverty,
The robust breast presses against
An iron world in love for multitudes.

Your motion was of man, your cry of woman's.
Your spirit moved like fingers
On a loom making coverings for
Innocence and secret shame;
Then the carrion came to fill the cup of gall.

What witness sign can hand make
That truly we did dwell in one house?
The false burdens now I bear
Make me living captive
In your domain of hunger.

You sang me songs of work and cleanliness
While your body began its burning.
Together we embroidered creeds.
The face of courage is my shield bequeathed;
With it I run to meet mine enemies.

Solitary am I a daughter of Zion,
Your inner and outer garments receiving.
Your forbear and invader,
I accept your purse and legacy of pictures,
Children, sucklings all my own.

The grave is filled with loam,
The seven chant as they exit from the park
Of dead; I enter your shadow
And make more dark its body.
The slap of universe claps across
The face of growth.
My father sits there wailing.

"How is the gold become dim!"
The stone becomes as an earthen pitcher.
I pour the quiver of my anger in it.

---

*A "Hes-ped" in Jewish tradition requires that mourners speak of the departed, especially of the good deeds.

COUSINS' CLUB

Tinkle and glass,
Where the silver shines.
The room Provincial,
Doubles by mirrors.

On the sofas the women
Sprawl like odalisques.
In the kitchen,
Fat runs off the slice of life.

The bushy-haired and the bosomed
Nest loud in the center;
The young in the corners chirp.

Bite the good sandwiches
And fling the confetti conversation.
Hurrah for us and for the family tree!
Speak low of those that sleep in its shade;
Pick acorns of art, sex and politics.

Forget the envy, the enmities
Under the leaves of years.
Be smiling as sudden fruit.
Shed rage and poverty.
Turn off the bare bulb,
Play the colored lights.

Let the mystery of family begin.

1959

MEMORIAM

There is no music for the feet of death
To pace the walk to graves.
Memory is our pitch;
Love hums below the stave.

The portrait grief of pale or black
Is worn to fit a cry of pain;
The living sigh a guilty breath,
The rabbi's chant tatoos the rain.

Together and apart the people mourn.
Children lean to them like seashells held to ears.
A woman wails; some richness in our breast
Flows to us through her chemistry of tears.

1966

BY THE SEA

The shouts of joy are close to cries of fear.
We grasp the tether of our strength like seaweed;
For some unnamed deed we beg anointment.

The walls of waves rise and liquefy;
The carbonation of the foam swallows our feet.
A bubbling joke of universe on man
Spills as out of a vessel on the celebrants.

Unlocked canals of love and thirst flow over;
We sail like boats to our divinity;
Watermarked we call like cormorants,
Singing in our fear and wheeling.

A swimmer calls alarm—
Gulls and people shoreward swoop,
Returning to the fire of life;
To boys and men of brick-hued bodies
Racing like heroic runners to douse danger.

The swimmer, blue and prone, revives.
Sunlight in his eye,
He cries, thanking the Guard for life.

Then we return to our blanket world and striped cabana,
To the private hug under the umbrella
And the allowed nakedness,
Shared with spinsters and old men eating sandwiches,
Where all but children sit,
Watching the limbo of their bodies
In the passage to Paradise.

1965

WASTREL

He had a bristled face
And landlord look,
But his land lay waste
        and weeds waned high
Up until the cobwebbed barn
Where the two-day calf stood calling.

His fuel was strewn
        and plows lay rusted.
Spare and stubbled was his estate
Where it might have preened
Rich as worms in the dark soil.

Only his cats thrived,
Sitting on a signpost facing west.

He sprawled on his land like Claudius
As we talked,
Falling anywhere like misfortune,
And told of laying hens,
And private winters
Full of husbanded amour.

I wondered how he came to farm
For eighteen years and still unreaped.

He seemed to ask a cloud,
And with a turning hand,
Paging this time and place, said,
"I used to be an actor,"
Then spat hard upon the ground.

1965

THE PLEASURE OF BEING HUMAN

The pleasure of being human:
To inhale,
And make thought billow into action
As a muscle bends.

To swirl a journey around the mind's earth,
To remember history and fear the future.

To sit two-footed as a king on throne,
And echo the petal of vowels
Like fronds falling;
A universe of flowers.
To sweat through skin;
To touch and receive a body.
To drop tears
And feel deep as waters teeming.

To flick one's fingers, then smiling,
Stand in the sun of humantide
Where light falls as if on stalks standing.

1964

THE FAMILY AT THE FALLOUT SHELTER

The family at the fallout shelter are mannequins;
True people pale at playing such a show.
They have dressed the dolls
In helmets red and white and blue.
(Protect the vault of thought at every cost.)
For loving, waiting, comforting, a couch,
And books to guard against insanity.
Fed they will be from pills, o patriots,
In that republic of caves
Whose walls will bear our artifact.

Alert! Alert! cries out the heart,
Run away and wail with sirens!
Call "Danger—Danger!"
Before the cosmic breath exhales,
Assume a soul,
Shout human, stricken with the plague of death,
And naked, plead to the machine for mercy.

1963

ABOARD THE *HONEY FITZ*

Thurs. April 26, 1962
News Item: Pres. Kennedy received word at
1:20 p.m. of the first atmospheric nuclear
test while cruising aboard his yacht, the
Honey Fitz. . . . Mr. K. was briefed this
morning by his naval aide; then he set
sail with his brother, Edward Kennedy,
and Mr. and Mrs. Randolph Hearst.

      While away down the bay
      While the operation's done
      We thought you'd kneel to pray
      Or scan books for words fine-spun.

      Give it two minutes of silence, please,
      And slow the engines down.
      You need not drop an anchor
      But try and listen for a sound
      Of sorrow in the cry of gulls,
      And smell the sulphur boiling.

      Rock like a demented mother ailing
      At the loss of children,
      Unscalped by Indians,
      Pioneer of the New Frontier.
      Now see your face
      In the mirror of the lake.
      Gone is the folk hero.
      Act out the Greek agony.

      Primeval joke aboard the *Honey Fitz*
      We are with you
      In this neolithic *sitz*
      As we stream along with you
      In our cruise down the eternal.

      And the weather never interfered.

ABSOLUTION

*July 1960 news item: Negro boys and girls
clad in white bathing suits used public pools
for the first time in North Carolina. There
was no incident, the Negro swimmers keeping to
themselves in a corner of the pool.*

Washed in the blood of the Lamb,
Hosanna,
Baptized in white today, O Lord,
So long waiting to drink
From your dry dry gourd.

White man's mercy falls like manna,
His judgment rains like God,
Holy holy Carolina,
Broken is the ancient sword.

North the rivers rush like Tigris,
South Euphrates joins her sea,
Immersing now like pilgrims in the Ganges,
Over sins the healing water poured.

Bitter is the taste of salt in summer,
White as suits and dark as fear.
The tide of crisis tears away the moss,
Revealing rock where strength was stored.

AUTUMN AGE

The leaves in Fall
Are rolled and grey and brown;
So like these are we
As the years fold down.

From summer verdant green,
Then yellow ash and coals,
Autumn with its flaming inks
Sends leaves to earth like scrolls.

The flow of days cascade,
The rustle of occasions;
As we in middle age,
They heap in noisy congregation.

Then listen to the wiser sound
Of quiet treads that press on leaves;
The days descend and syllables recede
From footfalls soft as season's thieves.

Soon winds play cruelly with the bony band
That sidewalks scratch, and like dead
Birds fall spent, till trampling makes
A whisper of the scene between our eyes and head.

1959

STUTTERER

His tongue chugged; his voice hissed
Like the whistle of a tardy train.
The celebrants awaited the refrain—
He rose and was a throttle letting steam.

At last the sentence rolled,
And each spooled off his brain
Exchanges comfortable as cream.

Hot and wet and waving like a flag,
He pricked our patience and unease,
But at the sputter of his flame
Our own thoughts teem.

1958

VALSE TRISTE

Let us go among
        great archways of the stores;
Let us buy rugs and buttons,
        perfumes and foreign shawls.

Let us stand holy
        at the ceremony of clothes
In windows.

Let us see the movie,
        swallow mints,
And taste the handsome danger
        of the heroes,
In this auricle
        where dull cells
Await pursuing hooves
        to stir the blood.

Let us wander in the aisles of time,
Small among the blazoned giants,
Where desires click on,
And speech is neon.

See then our small stairway,
With neat nooks and chairs as we go up,
Defeat the dizzy spans and wires,
The great sighing
        of the hung universe.

1958

SCRIPT FOR THE I.R.T.

The dusty I.R.T.
Peeling crusty rattlery,
Stitching all the miles of track,
Unwinding space as threads grow slack.

Bobbin jigs and breaks the seam,
We slip like silk toward tunnel's beam.
Busy busy needles stitch—
An end to mending; station's reached.

What is the cloth we rip, fast-spun,
From early light to evening sun.
To live is movement—having been,
To go, be seen, and make a din.

1954

TRIPTYCH FOR TALMUD TORAHS

I. *Deborah*

Here work calls to men;
Many labors of the hands
Fall to the little tailors.
Down all these streets
Wages send the fathers like unspooling thread.

The boys have made the sign:
Confirmed, and seals set on the hand and head.
The threshhold of the house is blessed.

Then girls with braids
Peep under the cover of the covenant;
An ancient prize too holy for their wiles,
They tongue the language and its prayer
And hear the storyteller's art.

Of such is migration's guile
That males must trade,
Though beards are kept
And caps are on the skull
Lest else a promise could annul.

Like Deborahs sitting under trees,
Dropping figs of philosophy,
The women chant the culture's song:
"Awake, awake, we are the shield,"
And stay the gentiles from the rear,
While husbands hold the front and genuflect.

II. *Melamed*

Ye shall come to the House of God that is Jacob:
Ye shall intone till the tongue curl.
Of fables have none!
Yea, the Books be your dwelling,
Such bounds are world enough.

Under this moon of change,
I cast my curses.
Adonai, Adonai!
Tremble before His name,
And to my own as seer.

I come not like Isaiah,
Though soon a prophet in my eyes
As pupils darken and down.
Repent! Rejoice!
You chanters of the Talmud,
For sins of exile weight the turning page.

III. *Moreh*

Moreh was the name I piped,
A child above your knee.
You stroked thoughts as hair,
My Genesis outran the Books.

Moreh was Saul and David;
Then Jacob, the coat of colors mine.
We lived the strength of legend;
One a shield, the other, star.

Moreh was liquid to the tongue
Where other names were ash;
The years of mind no flesh revealed
Save sculpture of a boy or man.

Moreh was close to bitterness, *moror*
When distanced from your moon.
Night steps then grew blind;
I tapped out time of numb.

On a certain day to a listener came,
To write new life on his coat of white;
I lay within a Joseph pit of past
And dreamed myself a standing sheaf.

The memory of your Scripture learned,
Untallised from the rabbi's bosoms
Is set upon my heart as secret seal;
Was it Talmud or Apocrypha?

1954

Melamed—"Learner"—a Teacher—traditional meaning
Moreh—Teacher—modern.

FOURTH OF JULY

Crisis peals in sudden sound:
  The moment is oval,
  Ready as a mouth.
Now the bell is bonged.
Like the heart's stroke,
Magnified,
Clanging at conscience.

Hear it sound, "truths self-evident,"
Bursting its steel;
"All men created equal,"
The people... the people.

Ring like a dream in our midst,
In Detroit, in Mobile,
Pause in Georgia,
Singing, "equal... equal..."

Intone the bells to the assaulters,
"Dissolve the political bands,"
"Declare the causes,"
Let truth spread like a stain
Over the virus of man,
Making him leap as light,
With *sacred honor* and *certain right.*

The bell is rung,
Speaking its steel,
All men created equal,
The people, the people...

1954

SEND FORTH A RAVEN

Who is out in the reigning rain?
The giants and the insects,
The swimmers and the drowners
Lie in the majesty of water
Brimming the country's cup past thirst.

If only we could drink of history,
And be as Noah,
Filled with oceans,
Yet above the flood.

Subject as I am
To the tyranny of wicked days,
And something of a beast
Saved in its stall with food and warmth,
Yet human in my forty thousand days,
I send forth a raven.

1953

RADICAL SPEECH
in the time of Senator McCarthy

In days of combat,
   Disguise must hang
   Like khaki onto thought.
Codes are tapped out;
Each one swears fealty to the Lord;
Disloyal keyholes must be stopped.

Therefore, bold brave heart
   That quickens in alarm,
Become a quiet threshhold to the mind,
Where white swans for surrender
   Dip into the lake.
Elephant, become the worm;
   Hear insects in the grass
All running toward the sounds of war.

Avoid the risen figure on the hill,
   Or you will fall together with the target,
And hieroglyphic be the words
When cursing the cabal of country.

Let your eyes be glass,
And crawl into a snail;
Wrap yourself in plumage like the birds.
Of books have none,
Lest you carry messages.
Above all, do not speak, but twitter,
Or plainly call for food.

If like stricken man
You dare call,
Then only cry or shout.

1951

THEME FOR A SINGLE GIRL

You drift like a bottle
In the ocean of the city,
Believing you will be found
When the tides change
By one walking on the shore.

No more Circe singing on the rock,
Nor a chance to play athletic like a nymph in groves.
How to be seen in a city,
Living like an insect in a sliver of wood.

Perhaps revive embroidery
And good works,
Or minister to men with hands,
Like carding wool or baking bread;
Then bed with them in pastures.

Fingers instead press type keys
And fold chemises;
Caress cigarettes
And take the Sunday papers like endearment in the arms.

Hurry home now from the show
Where love beats wings against the screen,
And the eyes, riding tracks of sentences in subways,
Hear the journey's roar,
In which a mating voice implores.

Living thus with lacks but lease,
You take your pills and drink your ease.

1951

ALBUM

Your face looks up at me
From under glass.

As though in history you lie,
Some fated prince.

I see a shadow at the tree
Where you sang; a memory to harrass.

I hear a whisper of a bed unchaste,
Where fear, not joy, the moment limned.

The specter of your illness was a creed;
We fled to music, darkness, days of fast.

Like children at a game of life we played,
While death sat in our house and grinned.

How was it then that unlike Eve
I fell from knowledge into innocence?

And while the years inveigh
Against my rib, your image spins.

1950   St. Louis, Mo.

ENEMIES

With slow spider gait,
Constellation of casual greed
And purposed kill,
Heavy with drams of fertile intention,
The swarms come.

Unfleshed bone
And fecund food;
The rebel crumb
Cast off the loaf,
      They habitate.
A mote, stirring in a book,
      Odors them to revenge.
Cells are where they teem most
      And crash antennae.

Great is their lift,
And cunning their wings.
Observe their universe
And how they decay the kingdom
      And the idea.

1950

ANTHEM FOR 1950

Your press cries death; your capitals call war,
    My country tis of thee.

Squads storm; common men are walled in cells.
    Sweet land of liberty.

Golden eagles swoop; bones of patriots they gnaw.
    Of thee I sing.

Visions sung by Whitman; Paine and Lincoln led,
    Land where my fathers died,

Plains made fertile; labor hammering.
    Land of the pilgrims' pride,

Asia trembles; let no A-bomb shatter Red;
    From every mountainside let freedom ring!

BLUES SONG

(for Pete Seeger)
(Chant with banjo)

North, East, South, West,
Find the place where we can rest;
Shake down dust,
Slake all thirst,
Bring the most and get there first.

Cent, dime, lift, strain,
You gamble or you use your brain;
Loss or gain,
Shine or rain,
Your spirit wears a black man's chain.

Church, shave, show, beer,
It costs the same but you stay clear;
In the rear,
In second gear,
You go slow but still they jeer.

Sing, dance, play, act,
You perform and then they clap;
It's your knack
To smile back
And mock yourself with your own crack.

Dig, scrub, truck, clean,
You've got to work for bread and bean,
Pay is lean,
Boss is mean,
You never get the job you dream.

Bus, train, street, store,
A special seat, another door,
A certain law
They ignore;
It makes you bitter all the more.

Lie, beat, drag, frame,
A crime is done and you're to blame;
"What's your name—?"
It's the same—
Like beast, not man, they hunt us game.

Shack, room, flat, rent,
You've got to live inside a fence;
In tenements,
Jim-Crow pent,
You get that lonely outcast sense.

Think, know, write, speak,
In separate schools they make us meek,
We're not freaks,
Just freedom's cheats,
They hide us, then they say, "Go seek."

Bat, pitch, catch, slide,
Don't mix teams, stay on your side;
They want to hide
Our athletes' pride;
Our Ruths and Cobbs they won't abide.

Read, sign, check, poll,
The Constitution says to vote;
It's a joke
If you note
We pay a tax or it's revoked.

Hot, slow, sweet, loud,
Play the music for the crowd;
Our bill of wrongs
Makes our blues song—
White man, will it be for long?

1949 St. Louis, Mo.

TRAVEL

No seas, wind, choke of fog,
No rare botany;
The human glance
And view of provinces
The sole expanse.

Buy a destination
Far from mind and space
Of habit's expectation.
Swift—past to present is the race,
Progress of the hand or heart
Be lost in time's damnation.
Seek to act the travel episode like art,
To strike the match of your creation.

How the eye and mind omniscient,
The constant ash of old persist;
The winds of place do not inspire
To flame the selves sufficient.

1948

PORTRAIT OF HAROLD

He tore his page from life,
And begged to be uncounted;
He fled to numbers and their echo,
A realm without rage,
To airplanes and aloneness,
Or drank deep of sodas.

He sang a song of orphanage,
At being son without a father,
Then shot guns against the world,
For seeming husband to his mother.
The twisted lines of family he prized,
When cousins could be called as brothers.

Prodigal of parents and his people,
He laughed their Mosaic house down;
But on his guilty inner stage
Scenes of sacrifice he played,
Then sulked and ate to grow round,
And dared the world him love.

And many women in the dark
To his hugging yielded,
For he could charm with arts,
And promise them a merry bed,
But with no tenderness,
He then became a weapon
To punish his unloving mother.

In this ballad of revenge,
He yet stood with the denied,
And lent his shout and fist
To the angers in history,
Shielding races from the whip,
Though he had avoiding eyes,
Was fat, and had a small boy's lips.

1948

PICASSO STILL LIFE

The objects of innocence
Have been sheeted over.
The mirror and the oranges
Lay unposed in folds of death.

        The hollow mouth guitar
        Lies choked in dust.
        The gut is torn,
        Unplucked for pity's elegy.

And these the symbols
   the mind distills:
        The portrait of evil,
        Dimension of defeat:

A flower springs from stone
   Gray and green in mould;
Sharp toothed at the bars
Its petals gnaw for light,
The form distorted in denial.

        The bull defies decay
           the ultimate home
           the shadow
           rust.

Its skull sits by
        still iron
Clanks in the empty memory
        of the chain
        and cage
        the hobnail
        the key.

The horns rising
Show the old blood dried
From the goring of fighters.

Captive and keeper:
    The ghoul guards the flower
    Striking roots in soil of night.

    With the drip of time on growth
    It awaits in neverness,
    Imprisoned in surrender:
                  still life.

1947

JOURNEYSONG

My time is not of revelry,
Of cameo and tapestry,
No castle do I praise and yearn,
Where Flemish flame and color burn.

Nor have listeners trembled at my touch
For words that tinted like a brush,
Yet I ride the road in velvet, as with string,
To country and hour I minnesing:

The road lies broad and far,
Like fabric to the wheel,
Not concrete, but spread scarves
We hem beneath the wheel.

The deadwood towns are lost
In rapid window sight,
The creek and track are crossed
In roller coaster flight.

The heaven's supple cheek
Is laid against the land;
The sun lifts on the peak,
The bridge of time is spanned.

I see ahead the pools
That seem a heat mirage,
My summer sense its wetness cools,
Then sudden dry, they dodge.

No mule meanders slow
Or winds through wagons flap,
Where pioneers to homesteads flowed,
We whip the prairie with a master crack.

The coursing in the blood
Thrums power like the car,
In liquid speed the muscles flood
And sweep us toward the evening star.

While dusk in figured vestment
Calls slowly with her horn of night,
The rails like strings of instrument
Receive the bow of evening light.

Brake and shift, step and lift,
No meter marks the leap and spin of heart,
To speed in space is man's own gift,
And with his journey sing his art.

1947, Kansas

NIGHT STEPS

Each to his pleasure bent
Goes walking on the pavement.

Some lonely with a cat at heels,
Others tasting solace in the cafes' meals.

Who hears the music of the time,
His motive right, obeying all the signs
That lead to place and chrome commodities,
Value under glass like oddities,
While middlemen stay home pursuing ends,
Regrooming, thinking business trends.

To a full moon in a wiser universe
We show our wound, as to a nurse.
Though bright the diagnostic tool
It cannot illumine the infested ill
That shows itself in sudden wanderings
To swarming places, secret journeyings
To remembered streets for retrospect
To see the silent children, then reflect.

Now, afflicted with the sickness Hope,
We revel in the parlor, dance and joke,
Shun the avenue innocent in light,
Endure, endure the lacks and night.

1946

ESQUIRE HILL

More perfect are their lamps than altar flame,
And holy on the threshold they might kneel;
The tables draped in ample cloth, unstained,
Hold rich the guilt they own but never feel.

The mirrors answer with their light the spoil,
And on the patio the master sprawls his day,
His titled rest from overseeing toil,
From clamors called in buying shares of hay.

The shout and surge of happening he hears,
Though dim his paper rings the world alarm,
The night of time will tick away the fears,
Redemption now enfolds him; he sleeps on.

And if his acre sounds the tread of hobo's heel,
If a wounded rabbit smears the sculptured lawn,
His Saint Bernard will have it for its meal,
Against trespassers they will sound the horn.

Contain this tenant and his nervous heart,
O pinewood floors and ivoryhandled door;
Soon the cat on the piano will strike a sharp,
Wind will blow from corners; mice will bore.

1946, Kansas City, Kansas

NUPTIALSONG
for Lois and Murray

From each his loneliness,
From each his private need,
Take each the slow fulfillment
That comes of joining soil and seed.

The fields of personal and world
On whose space the green did not arise,
Where indifferent yield turned rust,
The rich resource of love will thrive.

Take of one the surer tread of joy,
Her hands' dispatch and running tongue,
Her emphasis in eyes and wit's reunion.
Of his, take substanced mind
That dreams a partnership of men,
And dares assail an ancient fate.
Your emblems joined become estate.

The voice intones a lyric ritual,
The lavish rose unfolds to your embrace;
The chants of Solomon invoke the joy
That trembles in the body of the race.

May this day be horizon for your sight,
As season's readiness to land;
Together may you walk your earth
And work your harvest hand in hand.

1946, Lawrence, Kansas

OUTSIDER

We cannot cut away our raveled cloth,
And think to hide our shabbiness;
Though we enter the halls by stealth,
The hands, the hunger, will profess.

We cannot sit the portrait pose
And rest beneath the moneyed shade;
The lens reveals the hair of innocence
Among the frowning heads of gray.

Imposter in such company,
With fans their protests clack about,
"She comes customless from unsociety—
Will she shrink before we dare to rout?"

Chairs are winged in English rooms,
Pioneers look down from gilded frames,
Silos of wheat have bought the silver spoons,
The attic holds the rust and stains.

A visitor and with an alien name,
The New York Jew may only look.
Outside, my heart is unashamed,
Warmed by the hand that holds a book.

1946, Lawrence, Kansas

SUNDAY

Cubes of grass lay like plans from window view.
This is to be believed;
The true working of the time,
Its sounds the turning of legal papers.

My eyes hold the globe of day,
A child counting the mirrored forms;

A church in the hill
Stuck like a needle.
The people leaving,
Bright marbles rolling,
The hymn singing above:
Ave, Ave, on a harmonica.

A red dog trundles
Across the showered gutter.
The yellow pump at the edge
Is a blind dwarf;
He guards the town against impurity.

The boys, aimless in blue and brown
Shuffle on corners.

A family, like dancers,
Gesture greetings.
Compose the pastel group of Sunday
Ready for framing.

Only the birds leave earth;
The trees weaving looms of green in the wind
Ignore the sleeping street.

Within I move subtle as a squirrel,
Arranging person and thing,
And in books my mind
Follows the sober travel of beetles.

1945

A SUITE TO SCHOLARS
To Brooklyn College

1. Admission

First, arising from ocean of sleep,
Where dipped in dream's ablution,
I come forward crystal to the day
In clear beginnings.

Or dark tide in a phantomed time
Grows moss upon the rock of mind,
And serpents glint, vying to outswim;
But I escape the giant wave,
Awake!

Then in avenues,
Sinuous, streaming to the catch like fish,
A willing school runs upward.
Florid and flush
Crack the slapped colors;
On eager breasts,
On hips' spread softness.
Bright as on billboards
The lip is graven red,
The face is processed,
Product durable and fresh.

Rapid heartbeat, jocose crowd,
Shoulder brush and thicket brow,
Hard truths tossed like marbles
Click rival each to other.
My game is played for winning.
Then take your chance, brother.

Now to the campus lap
Between the land's hard knees
We climb to stay,
Late lulled and rocked,
Now for learning's legend being read.

The buildings,
Cubic in comfort, await.
Only the time in the tower
Will indicate
The circle complete,
Lead our movement in its orbit.
This is our arena for the years.
To wrest with tigers of mischance
While labials of bells
Lilt like petals on the air,
Set clef and key
To play our inner chord,
And sing the lyric good of art and history.
Here we might study only lines on wisdom's forehead,
Or like lovers, leave our kiss thereon.

2. Curriculum

The signed arrival,
The welcome in the fold;
Our stern fathers scorn in tutoring,
Their brooding brows
The area profound,
Preserving shadows
From the glare of inquiry.
While others,
The good brothers,
Smile us to simplicity,
Chalk our course
To sail the small idea
Like toy boats down our calm.

Enter the academy,
A listener;
Thinking crux is made
In midsts like these.

The few perceive,
And most hear it
Like a noise in distant cities.

See knitters of a cloth
Loving the intricate stitch;
Rhythmed gossipers,
We strive to weave
Their winding trick.
Along the corridor,
From the exalted door,
The halls of lecture,
Hear hum of discipline;
Chanters of scripture
To a lost religion.

And who will ask the name of book,
The rule and rigor,
What is the exercise
To stir us into meaning's elixir?
Then, the easy plans
The curve of graphs,
Column, note and fact
Spread for eyes' surmise.
They ask:
Equate significance
Into the shortest word.

We seek the gentlemen of affirmation,
Gather in the parable and epigram
And turn our raveled edge
With the quick seam of intelligence.
Parallel in our paths,
With mental profit,
Pursue our courses,
Tickertape the credits in our heads.
All is possession here.

There is no journey
But the freight of memory.
Not yet the mating of knowledge and self,
The liquid losing and joining.
Time in the tower indicates
The only circle complete.
We lead our movement
In its orbit.

Enter again:
Hear lyric good of art and history:
Passions dashed from lip to lip,
In book, in song, in poem;
The globe of feeling
Curving in the play's compass.
Brash march of figured kings,
Structure of men in centuries,
Phrases like the moist seal
Where the cup was set,
Leaving stain of our rebellion there.
The venom of denial,
The lionhead of wrath
Roaring in the ages' space.
The vast vengeance of eternity
In appointed death.
All these the sounds of page.

Then, tangent to our wish,
Seek the sciences,
Thinking its strict rod
Rules the kingdom absolute,
The country of no error
Where potentate is proof.
Hold the mirror up to matter,
And with the hammered argument

Shatter our vanity—
Not we the finite mineral
Most crystal in our being.
Touch specimens of ages,
Of prime man imprisoned in his ribs,
How with magic and shock,
Then defiant of gods,
He shaped his own wonderment.

But the master and the rod
Intones the rule, the catalog.
The sign and number
Cancels the cabal,
Radius and ratio
Divide constant and variable.
The squire principles the wheel,
Angles live within the sphere,
Logic tight in tables
Looks on.

3. Text

Soon falls the haze and darkness,
The vigor of day breathes out,
The cruel edge blunts,
The dimensioned sight dissolves.
All thrust and muscle of the hours
Now retreats to skull.
Night gathers in its cowl
Over the private need,
And in the grey clothed time,
Clangs its bell at conscience.

All dialog and proverb,
All voice as orator,
Not wisdom's formula,

A secret buried with the Greek,
Yet for us the word italic,
The unwrit didactic,
We have seen the album of antique.

With Heraclitus we have trembled
At the change and changing,
With Lucretius asked the faith,
The truth and error ranging.
All disciple and philosophy
Not in pale Greek's peripety.
In the morn of time
In their mindstream bathed,
Now, at the zenith,
We must make our sages.

Soon the spirit's renaissance;
We leave the ghosted hood and myth,
Beyond the mound and the bronze,
After battles on the tablets writ.
Then to make our epics, frescoes,
And architect the ways of men.
No dome for chosen wise,
No tower for lone philosopher.

Long walked mind
As fictive spirit behind.
Soul, the shadow of man, rise up,
We stand in the noon of human sun.

1945

NEW POET TO OLD

(on reading Robert Frost)

He seems to shun
   This age when things are done,
When from wounds of time blood has run.
   His life is one long thinking afternoon,
Taking notes on sun and moon.

He seeks a prophecy
In rare moth's wing,
And, finding dust in pockets
Writes lines on the millennium.

His is a search for specific:
The precise trill of whipporwill,
The undercurrent of *now* and *still*,
A symbol in a microscopic speck,
All things brief as a spent breath.

A grandfather in a twilight pose,
His mind with simplicity shows
The utter good of evening,
The still excursion under stars,
After days which as dried leaves are burning.

In these things he has a part:
The smell of death between hunter and gun
Outracing a deer in the winter sun,
The quality of heart
Between silent neighbors,
The zealousness of worms
At undermining earth,
The strength of hair and grass
As silently they grow in graves.

But what are epitaphs
Or delight of secret country paths
When an age has an engineering eye
And vision leaps as with the span of bridges.
We are still in thrall
With beasts and angels,
And in a crimsoned world of combat
Come forward in a cleansing wave.
The future is cupped in our bringing palms,
With infinite love we have steeled our arms.

Old poet,
The thrush is not supreme,
And harking and halting on tiptoe
Drowns in a midnight dream.
Out of the blunt hunger of thunder,
The dark eruption of guns,
Hear the flute call of morning
Growing like veins of body
Over the grandeur of land.
Soon we will cease and still the storming
And come out of our hard house
To stand for history in heroic story,
Cool and free with building hands.

And will you, old poet,
Lover of landscape,
Whittler of word,
Wander through our firmament
Still looking for your bird?

1945

LOVE POEM

(After John Donne)

Come, let us look out the window of our love.
If your eyes view by it, then does the spectrum bend
To borrow from your gaze the light it covets,
With which your features' radiance does contend.

So like the clear substance are our hearts,
Angels' spirit stain in us their hue.
Thus we have become in passion's art
A window in love's house all vision through.

And worthier yet than souls in stormy pilotry,
Are we as wandering craft in love's clear night,
When we view our beam of constancy
In faith's window, grief's elements drown their spite.

When I see the world through this illumined frame,
I am possessed of holy clarity;
But some friends looking in might name
It flesh, blind to its substance: rarity.

1944

A PICTURE FROM ITALY
for S.S.

War is the watchword of your guarding hand,
And joy the running promise of your soldier's laugh.
You there, in the gloom of Italian shade
Breathing on tender Maria who grows into eight.

Even the lens linger on child and man,
Smoothing her sapling knees,
Tilting her new blade's lean,
Askance, she looks from the sodden ground
Wondering how it is to be seen.

From the arbor's edge,
(I think of its ruined sight)
A trellis stares through the leaves
And sieves quintessences of light.

This is the scene gladdening the long year,
And gazing, I draw its yield:

> Beyond and down we run, all three,
> Away from the bomb, from the splintered tree,
> Into the grotto where olives are ripe,
> To stir in the leaves and scatter the mice.
> Shall we sew the tatters and sandal your feet
> Then time a race to the almond tree...

> Oh, if we were magic
> And the cannon would stop,
> We'd twine together in braids,
> Three strands in your lock.
> But we must sing, *Maria va l'recovero*,
> And put away the refrain *di primavera*.

You there, the man in the tableau,
Not framed in another time
Though rendered in Leonardo's hour,
This must be your portrait—
The outward heart of soldier-poet,
The moment of present proof
Coaxing the future:
Two of the new renaissance
Shaming the conqueror.

This, in a picture from Italy,
Not to fade, to forget in pockets.

1944

SPACE AGE

on reading James Joyce

Like shapes of rough bread,
The night clouds come as repast,
And from within,
    the home of fictive men,
I might, as one of them,
    lift wine, give goodness up
    in hands,
And trembling, turn Bible pages.

We have done with days' wooden ways,
The goings in the narrow lanes,
Have we done with bargain in the
    channels and the valleys
    and the straits,
To tincture with our tissue
In this sky,
Globing round us like a vast embrace,
Until we touch the last mineral of the sun
Veining the coiling heaven hair.

How live content within this space?
Here are fierce sounds of worlds uncreate.

1944

OVER A BRIDGE

Cathedrals look best in such a mist,
Etched with spirit and heaven hope.
The vowel of their bells still sing,
Prolonged in grey folds of stone.

At eight the blueness of air is all,
Throat-full and eye-deep.
The lamps of waking windows
Quiver like expanding tears
Hidden in the lid of sleep.

And feel how the train trembles:
An acrobat perilous
On the arms of athlete,
The bridge astride two shores
And the steel shoulders confident.

1944

TIMES SQUARE

People by people:
        from single digit man
        carried to decimal place:
        move over, multiply
Face by face.

Block by block
        turns the gaudy carousel.
        the colors curve and reel,
        brass horn laughter
World is on a wheel.

No radii, no hub
        we travel at the edge,
        rotate on pleasure's axis
        cafe coin greeting:
Space over time in taxis.

Its name is formula,
        cool concept of circumference
        describing equilibrium,
        not a square or circle
But said in human sum.

1943

LINES AT TWENTY-SIX

to H.A.

This was to be the time when I became your kind.
My clock at noon, myself now shaped
On wheel of learning; when the quarried mind
Its first stone image had undraped.
As a child I copied skill and rules,
And thought that triumph could be taught,
But when I grasped life's hammer and its tools
A storied pediment could not be wrought.
Nature's frame holds all the forms of art,
But none by passing time revealed.
The bronze of being is poured within the heart
Where feelings force the metal's yield.
    This time of yearly ripening is thus true,
    If only the rough stone of selves we hew.

1935

excerpts from
one act plays in verse

A HAMMER FOR THE WISE MAN

and

TIME OUT OF JOINT: A play for Shakespeare's birthday

Exmonides, the magician, is talking to a group of passengers who wait on the subway platform at midnight. Though he addresses all of them, he directs himself to Nina, the dancer, whom he has known from the past, and who now stands aloof from the group:

My occupation's magic, they all say,
Flip hats for rabbits, conjure cards and coin,
Turn water into fire and flame to ice,
Hide billiard balls and birds inside my mouth
And dance to any penny piper's tune.
But years ago, it seems like yesterday,
I lived within a constant miracle
Without the brass and smoke of cheap display.
I was a man novitiate and clean,
My youth and purpose made the steady sign
On life's horizon. Faith was progress:
Some with goods and labor, mine with art;
Greed and ignorance with patience would dissolve
When our leaders struck upon time's rock.
But whatever heaven's spirit once I had
Must have burned in devil's fires I made
Of anger in my heart and brain. O, Nina,
Man is herd and seeks the grass and root,
Lowly as the driven beast, his sight to ground,
Bed and food are answer, circumstance his master,
Movements and crusades only plots for authors—
Action and belief mark fools and angels!

Years in Europe I hoped that out of horror
Men would stir. At the turning spits
I saw them tied, made flesh for captors.
In prison there I searched my soul and cell
For some answer sprung from stone.
In that iron year I would pound and probe
As with a hammer, beating down the doubt,
But never did I find the grain of faith again.
Not like nature does man resume his seasons.
Once gone, his summer sleeps and dies in time,
But Fall of truth and hope before him lives.

Now I am like all who drowse their days,
Who hide in shells for warmth, secure from shock,
Who are slaked of sense and tasting food or thought
That in the orchards sinks unbitten down.
I have joined with those who visit here and there,
Those who with their clothes and trinkets
Play the rich who cherish coin and place,
Thinking thus to pass from page to page
With fading flourish in their grey history.
I am not one of them, nor yet myself—
My cloak wraps shades of magic will that are not there,
My circle's power lives only on the stage.
Heart is a hollow drum and touch is dust.
The time is barren; men await the rust.

TIME OUT OF JOINT ends with a declaration by Sir Francis Bacon, inadvertently unearthed by a gravedigger under Puck's influence, instead of Shakespeare; Bacon is speaking to Puck:

Be done now with this quarrel,
For it has the taste of sorrel
Too long pickled in the brine
Where divers authors long have lain.
All who claim our Shakespeare's brain
These three hundred years in theory's court,
Like gabblers argue cases, long and short—
For Raleigh, Rutland, Derby, Marlowe,
And Francis Bacon—all impossible to swallow...
As strange to me as rough-hewn carpentry
Would be a talent for plays and poetry.
My food and drink was science and philosophy,
And only William Shakespeare in his heart
Knew well the secret of his art.
Each, as you, Puck, in his special touch
Makes essence for the world to judge.
As surely as the kingdom goes the rose,
In one a king, the other, perfume, blows.
Be done with questions of the tidy mind,
The bone is sure but never sight from hind...
This William Shakespeare was a man above them all,
And like you he stood in a common stall;
His life was gentle, and the elements
So mixed in him that Nature stands up now
To say to all the world: *There was such a man.*
Though conspirators acclaim me, Francis Bacon, on his throne
I thrice refused a crown that is for Shakespeare's brow alone!

(Bacon begins to exit, then turns back to Puck.)

Now leave me, Puck, to worms and wood and woes,
For I have work in other worlds, of fire and ice that glows...

DORIS B. GOLD

is a native New Yorker who has lived in the Midwest. She has a B.A. from Brooklyn College and an M.A. in American Literature from Washington University, St. Louis, Mo.

She has taught English in Midwestern and Eastern schools. As a freelance writer, her reportage, human interest articles, reviews and feminist critiques have appeared in various magazines and newspapers. She has also worked as an editor, a community organizer, a social service administrator, and in public relations, both in New York City and the Midwest.

She has edited and written stories for children in the "Young Judaean" magazine, and in her book, *Stories for Jewish Juniors*, published by Jonathan David, 1967. Her essay, "Women and Voluntarism," appeared in *Woman in Sexist Society,* edited by V. Gornick and B. Moran, Basic Books, N.Y., 1971.

She has lived in Levittown, Long Island, and in Queens, N.Y. with her husband and two sons.

HONEY IN THE LION is her first collection of poems.

Temple Israel
Minneapolis, Minnesota

DONATED BY
KENNETH A. LAKE